1 MONTH OF
FREE
READING

at
www.ForgottenBooks.com

By purchasing this book you are eligible for one month membership to ForgottenBooks.com, giving you unlimited access to our entire collection of over 1,000,000 titles via our web site and mobile apps.

To claim your free month visit:
www.forgottenbooks.com/free891303

ISBN 978-0-265-79959-8
PIBN 10891303

This book is a reproduction of an important historical work. Forgotten Books uses
state-of-the-art technology to digitally reconstruct the work, preserving the original format
whilst repairing imperfections present in the aged copy. In rare cases, an imperfection in
the original, such as a blemish or missing page, may be replicated in our edition. We do,
however, repair the vast majority of imperfections successfully; any imperfections that
remain are intentionally left to preserve the state of such historical works.

Historic, Archive Document

Do not assume content reflects current
scientific knowledge, policies, or practices.

JAMES CURETON, Proprietor

GROWER OF A GENERAL LINE OF

Fine Fruit, Shade and Ornamental Trees Plants, Etc.

AUSTELL, GEORGIA

A Word to Our Customers

It has always been our ambition and purpose to maintain a reputation for growing and marketing the highest class of nursery stock that experience and conscientious care can produce. It is our aim to keep our field work, our packing and our shipping so well organized that mistakes may be reduced to a minimum.

OUR LOCATION—Austell is located in Cobb County, on the Southern Railroad, and close to Atlanta. Shipping facilities are the best to be had and there will be no delay in getting stock to any part of the country.

BUYING FROM CATALOG is growing in popularity year by year, and we earnestly desire to encourage our patrons to place their orders under this plan. Each order sent us by mail will receive personal care, will be packed securely in bale or box. On orders coming to us from far away states a liberal express or freight allowance will be made to apply on transportation charges. We guarantee safe arrival of every tree or plant, no matter where shipped.

PRICES NET CASH—Our prices are net cash. What others offer in discounts we guarantee in class of stock and superiority of service. We know of a fact that the net prices named in this catalog are as cheap as first-class stock can be bought in the United States, and we know further that agents' commissions are figured out of these prices rather than in them. We have eliminated the cost of the "middle man" in preparing these prices, a thing not heretofore done in the nursery trade.

GUARANTEE OF GENUINENESS—We use constant care in keeping trees true to name. Mistakes are avoided in every possible way, but when they do occur and we are notified of such mistakes, we gladly correct them, and if any stock proves not true to name we will replace it with the genuine or refund purchase price paid for same, but it is mutually agreed between purchaser and ourselves that we are not to be held liable for a greater amount than the original price paid for goods.

Suitable Distance for Planting

Apples, Standard............30 to 40 feet	Grapes	8 to 10 feet
Apples, Dwarf .... 8 to 10 feet	Currants	3 to 4 feet
Pears, Standard ....18 to 20 feet	Gooseberries	3 to 4 feet
Pears, Dwarf ....10 feet	Raspberries, Red	3 to 4 feet
Peaches ....16 to 18 feet	Raspberries, Black	4 to 5 feet
Nectarines and Apricots ....16 to 18 feet	Blackberries	5 to 7 feet
Cherries, Sweet ....18 to 20 feet	Strawberries, rows ......1 by 3½ feet	
Cherries, Sour ....15 to 18 feet	Strawberries, in beds......1½ by 1½ feet	
Plums ....16 to 20 feet	Asparagus, in beds ....1 by 1½ feet	
Quinces ....10 to 12 feet	Asparagus, in field.......1 by 3 feet	

Fruit Department

Apples

The Apple is the first in importance of all fruits. It will thrive on nearly any well-drained soil. Its period of ripening, unlike other fruits, extends nearly through the whole year. By making careful selection, a constant succession can be obtained. For family use there is no fruit that is more indispensable. No fruit is so healthful, and many physicians say that if a person would eat an apple a day they could dispense with doctor bills. Besides this, and just as important, is the fact that the average price on the market is steadily increasing and the immense demand for home consumption, foreign shipping, canning and evaporating assures high prices. The apple, if given the same care and attention as other farm crops, will yield greater returns per acre. The following list we consider to be the best for general planting.

Price of Trees

	Each	Dozen	100	1000
Two years, 5 to 7 ft.	$0.25	$2.50	$17.50	$125.00
Two years, 4 to 5 ft.	.20	2.00	12.50	100.00
One year, 3½ to 4½ ft.	.15	1.50	10.00	75.00
One year, 2½ to 3½ ft.	.10	1.00	7.00	50.00

Summer Apples

Carolina Red June—Medium size, red; its flesh is white, tender, juicy, sub-acid and an abundant bearer. June.

Early Harvest—Size medium, roundish, is usually more or less oblate; bright straw color when ripe; flesh nearly white and flavor rather acid; ripens early and continues for about three weeks afterwards. Productive.

Early Yellow May (Juneating)—Small and round, sometimes oblate, smooth, regular; pale greenish-yellow, russet around stalk; tender, sub-acid. Ripens before Yellow Harvest.

Early Red Margaret (Southern Striped June)—Medium, round-ovate; striped with dull red, somewhat russeted; flesh sub-acid, tender, good when fresh. Ripens at wheat harvest; moderate bearer.

Horse—Large, varying from oblate to round, ribbed, yellow; flesh rather coarse, sub-acid; tree vigorous, productive. A fine summer cooking apple; also good drying apple.

Stayman's Winesap.

5

Hackworth—Origin Alabama. Medium to large, very aromatic, granular yellow flesh, striped with red splashes. One of the best apples. Ripens in July and August.

Red June.

Red Astrachan—Free growth, large, roundish, deep crimson; juicy, rather acid, good; very hardy. Highly esteemed on account of its very fine appearance, earliness and hardiness. Ripening in August.

Sweet June—Rather small, roundish, regular; skin smooth, light yellow; flesh yellowish, very sweet, rich; tree upright, vigorous, productive. Valuable summer sweet apple.

Yellow June (Kirkbridge White)—Medium oval, tapering to apex and base, equally blunt at both ends; smooth, pale yellow, flesh very tender, fine grained, sub-acid flavor. Ripens after Early Harvest. Great bearer, too tender for long transportation.

Yellow Transparent—Medium size, roundish, slightly conical; pale yellow when fully mature; tender, juicy, sprightly sub-acid; good. August.

Autumn Apples

All Summer—Rather small, roundish, and greenish-white; flesh white, crisp, pleasant. July and August.

Carolina Greening (Green Cheese)—Size is medium, oblate; green in the shade, red in the sun; flesh crisp, tender, delicate; a fine fall apple; resembles Fall Cheese, but keeps longer.

Grimes' Golden—Medium, skin rich golden yellow; flesh white, tender, juicy, with a peculiar aroma; tree a good grower and an early bearer. A very papular sort.

Morrison's Tenderskin—Small, yellow and striped; tender, pleasant and sub-acid flavor; very good. Early winter. Southern.

Winter Apples

Arkansas Black—Large, round or slightly conical; regular, smooth, glossy yellow where not covered with deep crimson, almost black; flesh very yellow, firm, fine-grained, juicy; flavor sub-acid, pleasant, rich.

Albemarle Pippin or Yellow Newtown—Size large, round, a little lopsided, ribbed and irregular; tree a slow grower and light bearer, but rich soil and care will do wonders with it in the East and West.

Ben Davis—Origin, Kentucky. Season January to April. Vies with Baldwin as a profitable commercial variety in many sections. Quality not so good, but a better bearer and keeper. Tree very vigorous and hardy in the Central states. Fruit large, handsome, and brightly striped with red; flesh medium in quality.

Limbertwig, Improved (Coffelt) — Medium size, striped and splashed red. Good orchard tree; bears abundantly and regularly. The farmer's best keeping apple. Originated in Benton County, Ark., and is making good.

Delicious—Fine quality and flavor; red or striped red, shading to green at blossom end.

Fallawater (Fornwalder, Tulpehocken)—Is very large, globular; yellowish-green, dull red cheek; juicy, crisp, pleasant, sub-acid flavor; tree a strong grower; very productive, even while young. November to March.

General Taylor (Westbrook's Rough and Ready).

Gano—Originated in Missouri. Similar, but superior to Ben Davis. It has all the good qualities in a higher degree, more brilliant coloring, runs more even in size, and keeps fully as late. Tree is vigorous and hardy; is a rapid grower; bears while young. Color bright red, without stripes or blotches and large and even in size. Season February to March.

Jonathan—Medium size, of a deep red color; flesh very tender, juicy and rich; a very productive apple. One of the best varieties for the table, cooking or market. A very popular variety through the West.

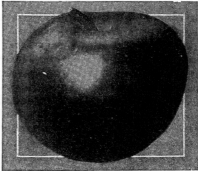

Rome Beauty.

King of Tompkins County — Large, handsome, striped red and yellow; tree vigorous and productive. One of the best sorts.

King David — Medium size, early winter apple of the Jonathan type; uniform shape, tapering to the blossom end, dark red, purplish black on sunny side when highly colored; flesh firm, tinged with yellow; crisp, juicy and good quality. A fine shipper; tree hardy and vigorous.

Kinnard's Choice—Medium oblate; yellow, covered with dark red; flesh tender and juicy; tree vigorous, hardy. Bears young.

Mammoth Black Twig—One of the most profitable and valuable on the market; resembles the Winesap, except that it is from one-third to one-half larger.

North Carolina Limbertwig — Well-known Southern variety, above medium size; color purplish red; flavor sub-acid, rich and aromatic. Productive and keeps well.

Rome Beauty—Large, roundish, and very slightly conical; mostly covered with bright red on pale yellow ground; flesh tender, not fine grained, juicy, of good quality. Ripens early in winter. The large size and beautiful appearance of this Ohio apple render it popular as an orchard variety.

Royal Limbertwig — Large, oblate; pale yellow, striped red; flesh yellow, rich and juicy.

Stayman Winesap—Is now attracting attention everywhere as a profitable market variety. Has large size, bright color, great productiveness and best quality to commend it. Tree is a vigorous grower and, like its parent, is irregular and drooping in habit, and adapts itself readily to different soils and situations. November to February.

Shockley—Medium, roundish-oblong, yellow striped and clouded with red; dark greenish russett blotches; flesh firm, of good flavor. October to March. Georgia.

Smoke House—Large, yellow, shaded with bright red; flesh firm, crisp, juicy and fine flavored. Especially esteemed in Pennsylvania. October to November.

Terry's Winter—Medium oblate, dark red; flesh yellow, crisp, sub-acid; good keeper; Georgia.

Wolf River—An apple peculiarly adapted to the West on account of its extreme hardiness; very large and handsome, flesh whitish, pleasant, sub-acid. A good bearer. November to December.

Winesap—Large; roundish; deep red; medium quality; keeps well. A good bearer; succeeds well in the West. December to May.

York Imperial—Tree moderate grower and productive; fruit large, lop-sided; surface smooth; color mixed, bright red on yellow ground; flesh yellowish, tender and juicy; flavor mild, sub-acid; quality very good. Season November till spring.

Yates—Small, oblate, yellow, covered with dark red striped, small white dots; flesh yellow, spicy, sub-acid. Great bearer and good keeper. Georgia.

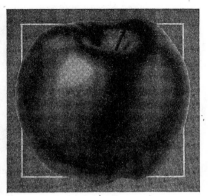

Delicious.

Special Apples

Prices of Trees.

	Each	Per Doz.	Per 100
Two years 5 to 7 ft.	$0.50	$5.00	$35.00
Two years 4 to 5 ft.	.40	3.50	25.00
One year 3½ to 4½ ft.	.30	3.00	20.00
One year 2½ to 3½ ft.	.20	2.00	15.00

Rabun Ball.

Whitley.

Taylor's Number 1.

Taylor's Number 2.

Taylor's Number 3.

Mitchell's Winter Russett.

Crab Apples

Prices of Trees.

	Each	Per Doz.	Per 100
Two years 4 to 6 ft.	$0.25	$2.50	$17.50
One year 3 to 4 ft.	.15	1.50	10.00

Hyslop—Tree is a moderate grower, making beautifully shaped, thrifty tree; bears young. Fruit large, nearly round, flattened at the ends, skin smooth; color dark rich red on yellow ground. Flavor very good.

Large Red Siberian—About an inch in diameter, grows in clusters; yellow, lively scarlet cheek, tree erect, vigorous, bears young and abundantly. September to October.

Transcendent—A beautiful variety of the Siberian Crab. Tree a strong grower and very productive, bearing the second year. Excellent for cooking and drying; good for cider, being crisp and juicy.

Yellow Siberian—Medium, round, golden yellow; vigorous grower. Ripens in September.

7

Peaches

In order to preserve the continued healthy growth of the trees and the fine quality of the fruit, the trees should have the shoots and branches shortened every few years, so as to preserve a round, vigorous head with plenty of young wood, and the land should not be seeded to grass, but kept in constant cultivation.

The following have been selected after an examination of many different sorts in bearing, the best only being chosen.

Prices of Trees, except where noted.	Each	Per Doz.	Per 100
One year 5 to 7 ft.	$0.20	$2.00	$12.00
One year 4 to 5 ft.	.15	1.50	10.00
One year 3 to 4 ft.	.10	1.00	8.00

SC—Semi-cling. C—Cling. F—Freestone.

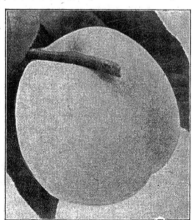

Crawford's Late.

Arp Beauty (F)—Color flesh yellow, mottled bright crimson. Excellent flavor, juicy. Tree good grower and productive.

Alexander (SC)—Medium size; greenish-white, nearly covered with rich red; flesh sweet and juicy; tree vigorous and productive; a good market peach.

Admiral Dewey (F)—A perfect freestone, of fine size, form and color, with delicious yellow flesh, that is yet firm enough to ship well. The tree is a strong, hardy, symmetrical grower that produces well. The very best early yellow freestones. July.

Belle of Georgia (F)—Very large, skin white, with red cheek; flesh white, firm and of excellent flavor; fruit uniformly large and showy. Tree a rapid grower and very productive. Early July.

Carman (F)—A new, hardy, rot-proof peach. Large, round, pale yellow skin and red blush on sunny side; white flesh, sweet flavor.

Chinese Cling (C)—Large, globular; skin white, shaded with light red; flesh white, red at the stone; very juicy, melting and rich. July.

Crawford's Late (F)—Large, roundish-oval, yellow with broad red cheeks; flesh yellow with red at pit, melting, vinous and very good. Late September.

Emma (F)—A beautiful, very large peach; yellow with light crimson cheek; flesh yellow, fine grained, very juicy; quality best. Freestone. In maturity it follows immediately after the Elberta.

Early Rivers (SC)—Large, light, straw color, with delicate pink cheeks; flesh juicy and melting, with a very rich flavor. July 20th to August 1st.

Crawford's Early (F)—Large roundish, bright yellow with red cheeks; flesh yellow, juicy and sweet; quality good. August and September.

8

Flater's St. John (F)—Large, resembling Crawford, deep red; flesh yellow, good. Very early. Southern.

Greensboro. (SC)—The largest and most beautifully colored of all the early peaches. Of good quality, juicy, a freestone, but adheres slightly; ripens perfectly to the seed and with the Alexander, which makes it of great value as a market peach.

Governor Hogg (F)—Large white with blush. Flesh, white, tender, juicy, highly flavored; red at pit.

Helley (Early Belle) (F)—Large, white, red cheek, Early Georgia.

Indian or Blood Cling (C)—Large, dark claret, with deep red veins; downy; flesh deep red; very juicy, vinous and refreshing. Middle of August.

Lemon Cling (C)—Very large and beautiful lemon-shaped; light yellow with red in sun; flesh firm; yellow and rich, sub-acid flavor. August.

Lady Ingold (F)—Medium, red on yellow; flesh yellow, sweet, rich. Ripens one week earlier than Crawford's Early. North Carolina.

Mayflower (SC)—Earliest peach known. Ripens one week before Sneed; dark red all over; beatiful appearance, carries well to market. Blooms very late, crop never entirely cut off by frost. Size medium, quality good. Tree upright, good grower, very prolific bearer. Originated in Copiah County, Miss.

Mountain Rose (F)—Large, handsome; yellow with red cheeks; flesh white and juicy; one of the best. August.

Elberta.

Old Mixon Free (F)—Large; pale yellow with a deep red cheek; tender, rich and good. One of the best. First to the middle of September.

Old Mixon Cling (C)—Large, pale yellow with red cheeks; flesh juicy, rich and of high flavor; one of the best clingstone peaches.

Picquet's Late (F)—Very large; yellow; with red cheek, flesh yellow, buttery, rich, sweet and of the highest flavor. Maturity from end of August to middle of September. This variety seldom fails to produce a crop of fruit, one of the most prolific late yellow peaches South and West.

Raison—Originated in Coweta County, Ga., Indian type. Clingstone. Flesh stained red, very juicy, sweet, slightly vinous and rich. August and September.

Salway (F)—Large, roundish, deep yellow with rich red cheek.. flesh yellow, firm and juicy and sugary; a late market sort.

Stinson's October (C)—Medium, white with red cheek, excellent flavor. Profitable peach for late market.

Stonewall Jackson (C)—Like Lee's Cling. July 25th.

Sneed (SC)—Very early; fruit medium size, creamy white, with crimson blush. Ripens evenly, is firm; sweet. Productive.

Thurber (F)—Large, roundish, oblate, creamy white marbled with crimson; juicy; melting; rich; ripens in July in Georgia.

Victor (SC)—An early peach, ripening before Sneed. Tree good grower and immense bearer. Flesh greenish white, juicy; pleasant sub-acid flavor, semi-cling. Latter part of June.

Wonderful (F)—Large, round, somewhat oval; yellow with carmine blush; flesh yellow, tender, and high flavored; a good peach for home gardening or shipping; late.

Waddell (F)—This variety is largely planted commerecially in the South. It is a very good shipper and of good quality. Color creamy white with bright blush.

Peaches packed in box.

White English (C)—Large, creamy white with red cheek, juicy and sweet. Quality of the best. A reliable sort for home use or orchard planting.

Special Peaches

	Each	Per Doz.	Per 100
One year 5 to 6 ft.....	$0.50	$5.00	$30.00
One year 4 to 5 ft.....	.40	4.00	25.00

Corosa (SC).

Cureton's Late Free (F).

Early Wonder (SC).

Everbearing (F)—Medium white, vinous, juicy, good. No value for market.

Justice October (C).

Mary's Choice—A very productive, New Jersey peach, requires thinning and high culture.

Martin's (F)—September.

Malicatune Cling (C).

Pauline (F).

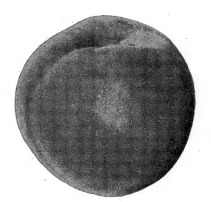

Early Crawford.

Apricots

Apricots succeed best in the western part of the country, but with careful handling the following varieties will be found profitable in the South for home and commercial planting. The Apricot should be planted same as the peach.

Prices of Trees.

	Each	Per Doz.	Per 100
Two years 5 to 7 ft....	$0.50	$5.00	$35.00
Two years 4 to 5 ft....	.30	3.00	20.00

Alexander (Russian)—Medium to small, light orange, yellow flecked with red; flesh tender, juicy, sweet and good quality; hardy; very productive. July.

Early Golden—Small, roundish-oval; pale orange with smooth skin; flesh yellow, juicy, sweet and of the best quality; hardy and productive. Freestone.

Moorpark—One of the largest; orange yellow with numerous specks and dots; flesh yellow, sweet, juicy, and rich; tree somewhat tender and inclined to ripen unevenly.

Superb—Seedling from Kansas. Best flavored, most productive. Quality is excellent; medium size; light salmon color.

Early Golden.

Quinces

The Quince is easy to grow if planted in soil where adapted. Over the South it should only be planted for home use. A few trees will prove profitable and for culinary purposes no fruit takes the place of the quince. Trees are of dwarfish growth and come into bearing very soon after planting. We can furnish in any grade the following varieties:

Prices of Trees.

	Each	Per Doz.	Per 100
Two years 4 to 5 ft....	$0.40	$4.00	$30.00
One year 3 to 4 ft....	.25	2.50	17.50

Apple or Orange—Large; roundish; with a short neck; bright golden yellow; very productive. This is the variety most extensively cultivated. September.

Angers or Quincedonia—Somewhat later than the preceding fruit, rather more acid, but looks as well. Tree a thrifty grower and abundant bearer.

Chinese—Very large, oblong, rather coarse; tree vigorous grower, but late bearer. Does best in the South.

Meech's Prolific—Very large, bright yellow, quality very good, quite fragrant; bears early and is quite productive. One of the best. Midsummer.

Rea's Mammoth—A seedling of the Orange Quince: one-third larger, of the same form and color; fair, handsome, equally as good and productive.

Pears

We cannot recommend too strongly the advisability of planting pear trees, both for home use and commercial orchards. Since the introduction of the hardiest varieties there is no section of this great country but that can have an abundance of this delicious fruit by exercising a little care in choosing varieties.

Prices of Trees.

	Each	Per Doz.	Per 100
Two Years, 5 ft. up	$0.35	$3.50	$25.00
One year, 4 ft. up	.25	2.50	17.50

Buerre d'Anjou—A large fine pear, buttery and melting with sprightly flavor; tree a fine grower and very productive. One of the best. October to January.

Bartlett—Large size with a beautiful blush next the tongue; buttery, very juicy and highly flavored, bears early and abundantly. Trees vigorous and very popular.

Clapp's Favorite—Very large, yellowish green to full yellow when ripe; marbled with dull red in the sun; covered with small specks; flesh melting and rich. Tree vigorous and good grower. Should be gathered early.

Duchess d'Angouleme—Very large greenish yellow, sometimes russetted; makes a beautiful tree and heavy bearer, buttery, melting and sweet. October and November.

Flemish Beauty—Tree generally preferred as a standard; fruit large, skin little rough, pale yellow, mostly covered with patches of russet, becoming reddish brown at maturity on the sunny side; flesh yellowish-white, juicy and rich. One of the best. September.

Garber—Large, bright yellow with red, juicy and good; a splendid canning pear, tree vigorous and hardy, not subject to blight. Ripens just after Bartlett.

Buerre d'Anjou.

Japan Golden Russet—Medium, russeted yellow, worthless for fruit, but tree very ornamental.

Kieffer Hybrid—This is a seedling raised from the Chinese Sand Pear crossed with the Bartlett. Skin rather tough, color yellow with red cheek in the sun. Fresh, white, juicy, buttery and rich. Tree is a very strong, upright grower. Very profitable for market

Koonce—Medium to large, very handsome, surface yellow, one side covered with bright carmine, dotted with brown; very early, quality good, spicy, juicy, sweet.

LeConte — Highly recommended; flesh melting, sweet, juicy, and aromatic; good sort for the South. Ripens about with Bartlett.

Magnolia (Japan Seedling)—Large, round, russety, firm; tree erect, hardy, vigorous; a late bloomer; very prolific.

Seckel—Small, rich yellowish-brown; one of the best and highest flavored pears known; very productive. September and October.

Wilder—Size medium; greenish yellow with brownish-red cheek and numerous dots, flesh white, fine grained, melting, excellent; about three weeks earlier than the Bartlett.

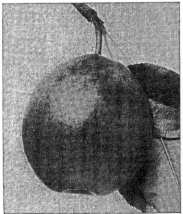

Kieffer.

Howell—One of the finest American pears. Large, handsome, sweet and melting; tree very vigorous, hardy and productive.

BURBANK

Plums

The Plum is becoming more popular in the South every year. Will grow fine wherever peaches are grown and require same character of cultivation, pruning, etc. The following list we have found to be the best.

PRICES OF TREES

	Each	Per Doz.	Per 100
Two years, 5 to 7 ft.	$0.35	$3.50	$25.00
Two years, 4 to 5 ft.	.25	2.50	17.50
One year, 3 to 4 ft.	.15	1.50	10.00

CHICKASAW TYPE

Wild Goose (Chickasaw Type)—The earliest good plum, large, bright red, with purplish bloom, a very good grower; bears early and abundantly; sweet and of a very good quality. July.

EUROPEAN TYPE

Shropshire Damson—One of the best for preserving, flesh amber colored; juicy and spicy; tree vigorous, hardy and an abundant bearer.

Imperial Gage—Above medium size; ovel pale green, tinted with yellow; very juicy and rich; fine for canning. Late July.

JAPANESE PLUMS

Abundance—One of the best Japan plums. Tree is a very rapid grower, healthy and comes into bearing quite young and yields abundantly; medium size, rich, bright cherry red with distinct bloom and highly flavored; flesh light yellow, juicy and tender, and excellent quality. Tree vigorous and hardy.

America—This giant plum originated from seed of the well-known "Robinson" from a cross with the Japanese plum, "Botan," and is from the same combination which produced "Gold" and "Juicy," both of which have proved generally hardy throughout the U. S., and no doubt "America" will prove quite as hardy. Color coral red.

Burbank—Large, globular, cherry-red, mottled with yellow color; flesh yellow, melting, juicy, sweet; semi-cling. One of the best. July 1st to 10th.

Chabot (Japan)—A splendid plum; flesh sweet and of an excellent flavor; ripens about the middle of August when all the other plums are gone.

Red June or Nogate—Medium to large; deep red with handsome bloom; flesh light lemon-yellow, juicy and of fine quality. Tree vigorous and productive. Ripens July and August.

Wickson—Large, heart-shaped, deep maroon red; flesh very firm, yellow, sub-acid, rich and good; a good shipping plum; tree upright but in some localities a shy bearer.

Cherries

Black Tartarian Cherries.

A great deal of attention is now given to the growing of Cherries. No home orchard is complete without its proportion of Cherry trees, and it is one of the most profitable market fruits. It will succeed on any kind of soil that is not wet.

Prices of Trees.

	Each	Per Doz.	Per 100
Two years 5 ft. up	$0.35	$3.00	$25.00
One year 4 ft. up	.25	2.50	17.50

Black Tartarian—Very large, bright purplish black, half tender, juicy, very rich. excellent flavor, productive, free. Ripens first to middle of July.

Black Heart (Sweet)—Very large; black, juicy, rich, excellent and moderately productive.

Early Richmond—An early red, acid cherry; very valuable for cooking early in the season. Ripens through June. A free grower, hardy, healthy, and very productive.

Gov. Wood—Clear light red, tender and delicious. Hangs well on the tree. End of June.

Napoleon—A magnificent cherry of the largest size; pale yellow with bright red cheeks; very firm, juicy and sweet, Bears enormous crops; ripens late, valuable for canning.

Wragg—Large, roundish, heart-shaped; dark crimson and when fully ripe, black or nearly so; flesh and juice light crimson, firm and good, very productive; one of the hardiest and is usually a sure cropper

Yellow Spanish—Vigorous growth, large; pale yellow with red cheeks; firm, juicy and delicious; very good. Ripening end of June.

Figs

Prices of Trees.

	Each	Per Doz.	Per 100
4 to 5 ft	$0.35	$3.00	$25.00
3 to 4 ft	.25	2.50	20.00
2 to 3 ft	.20	2.00	17.50
1 to 2 ft	.15	1.50	12.00

Brown Turkey—Large, very sweet, hardy, reliable. Color brownish purple.

Brunswick—Very large, white; productive and hardy.

Celestial—A small pale violet fruit; very sweet, prolific and hardy.

Green Ischia—Medium size, greenish-white when ripe. Flesh white, tinged with red. Good table variety.

Lemon—Fruit medium to large, flattened, slightly ribbed; yellow, flesh white, sweet; early. Strong grower and very prolific. A favorite for canning.

Magnolia—Fruit very large and of rich straw color. Begins to ripen the last of June and continues to put on new fruit until frost. Trees bear when quite young. Doubtless the most profitable variety grown.

Mission—Medium to large, skin rough—mahogany violet, with red flush; pulp red, sweet but not rich Profitable on account of its great productiveness.

Japan Persimmon

Prices of Trees.
Budded or Grafted

Heavy	Each	Per Doz.	Per 100
5 to 7 ft	$0.50	$5.00	$35.00
4 to 5 ft	.40	4.00	30.00
3 to 4 ft	.25	2.50	20.00

Among—Flattened like a tomato, with depressed apex, occasionally deep ribbed; extra large, skin dark, yellowish-red; flesh dull red with brown spots around the seeds of which there are sometimes a few. Very sweet and juicy; good keeper. September.

Hackiya—One of the largest and most showy; slightly conical and pointed. Skin bright crimson with lines around the marking at apex; flesh light. Tree vigorous and handsome. Moderate bearer. September.

Miyo-tan—Spherical or slightly elongated; diameter 2½ inches; skin orange red; flesh dark reddish brown; edible before softening. Ripens in October and keeps late.

Hiyakume—Large, round, generally flattened, but sometimes slightly elongated; 3 to 4 inches in diameter; skin yellow with network of lines around the apex; flesh dark, solid and sweet. Desirable for market. Last of September.

Concord
Grapes
from
Photo

Grape Vines

Grapes

No matter how small the home, one can usually find space for from four to six Grape Vines, which will bear an abundance of luscious fruit which cannot be surpassed. They can be trained over the garden fence, over the veranda, not only furnishing fruit, but making a vine that is beautiful and at the same time furnishing shade. Probably the best way to grow Grapes, however, is in rows, planting the vines from six to eight feet apart each way and training on trellis. Work the ground deep and well for Grape Vines, planting a little deeper than they stood in the nursery rows. Keep pruned severely for the first two or three years, allowing the vine to form four or five main stems, when later growth will suggest individual pruning. We again say plant the Grape, for both home and market, for no fruit will come nearer pleasing all tastes and adapting itself to all soils.

PRICES OF VINES

Prices of Vines.	Each	Per Doz.	Per 50	Per 100
Brighton	$0.10	$1.00	$3.00	$5.00
Berckmans Red	.10	1.00	3.00	5.00
Concord	.10	1.00	2.50	4.00
Catawba	.10	1.00	3.00	5.00
Colerain	.25	2.50		
Delaware	.15	1.50	3.50	6.00
Early Ohio	.15	1.50	3.50	6.00

	Each	Per Doz.	Per 50	Per 100
Green Mountain	.25	2.50		
Ives	.10	1.00	3.00	5.00
Lutie	.25	2.50		
Lucile	.25	2.50		
Moore's Early	.15	1.50		
Moore's Diamond	.15	1.50		
Niagara	.15	1.50	3.50	6.00
Worden	.15	1.50		

Brighton (Red)—Bunch medium to large, quite compact, flesh rich sweet and best quality, color dark crimson or brownish-red; vine vigorous and hardy.

Berckman's Red—Bunch medium, compact, round, dark wine color, flesh juicy, vinous, rich, pulp tender. Cross between Clinton and Delaware. Very good. September.

Concord (Black)—Bunch and berries large, round, black, thickly covered with a beautiful bloom; flesh moderately juicy, sweet pulp; quite tender when fully ripe.

Catawba (Red)—Branches medium, shouldered; berries large, deep coppery red, becoming purple when ripe; flesh somewhat pulpy, juicy, sweet, aromatic and rich; one of the latest; does not ripen well in North. North.

Colerain (Greenish Yellow)—A very fine grape of excellent quality, vigorous, heavy bearer, skin tender, very sweet and fine for table use.

Delaware (Red)—One of the best red grapes; bunch small and compact, berry small, vinous, sweet and delicious; best quality, good market grape.

Early Ohio (Black)—Briefly, its points of merit are extreme earliness, hardiness, and productiveness; berry is black, smaller than Concord; firm in texture; vine is thrifty, strong rapid grower and an abundant bearer. Its exceeding earliness makes it a decided acquisition.

Green Mountain (White)—Earliest white grape; bunch medium to large, shouldered; berries medium, greenish-white, tender, sweet, and excellent quality, combines hardiness, fruitfulness and vigor and health. A valuable sort.

Ives Seedling (Purple)—Healthy and a strong grower. Bunch and fruit medium to large. Flesh sweet and juicy, but foxy and puffy. Dark purple in color. July.

Lutie—Earliest in market; never known to rot; vine perfectly hardy, strong grower and enormously productive. Vines two years old from cuttings have produced each twenty-five pounds of fruit. Flavor equal to Delaware. Sweet and rich.

Lucile (Red)—Medium size, red, vigorous, hardy, productive. New.

Moore's Early (Black)—Bunch and berry large with blue bloom; quality better than

Concord.

Concord; its size and earliness render it desirable.

Moore's Diamond (White)—Bunch large, compact; berry medium size, color greenish-white with a yellow tinge, flesh juicy and almost without pulp. Very good. Vine vigorous and productive.

Niagara (White)—One of the leading white sorts; bunch large, shouldered, compact; berry large, yellowish-white, juicy, vinous and sprightly, quality good; skin tough, making it a good shipping and market berry.

Worden (Black) — Ripens a few days earlier than the Concord; bunch large and compact; berry large black, and of good quality. Vine vigorous and productive.

Grapes (Muscanine Type)

	Each	Per Doz.
Two years extra strong	$0.25	$2.50
One year extra strong	.15	1.50

Yellow Scuppernong—Bunches very small, loose; berries round, large; skin tender, juicy, sweet, musky. Valuable for the South.

James Grape (Purple)—Prolific; late.

Flowers (Black)—Bunch small, berry medium, round, black, sweet.

Thomas (Black)—Bunch small; berry large, oblong, transparent, violet; pulp tender, sweet, vinous. Southern.

Niagara.

15

Blackberries

When given a reasonable chance, they yield very abundantly and always find a ready sale at good prices. Unless planted in a sheltered location they should be covered with earth for winter in the North

Eldorado.

Price of Plants 10c each, 60c per dozen, $3.00 per hundred, $15.00 per thousand.

Eldorado—A valuable variety, medium size, jet black, melting, sweet and rich; hardy and very productive.

Kittatinny—Large, sometimes 1½ inches in length; glossy black; flesh moderately firm; canes are vigorous and hardy; very productive.

Rathbun—Strong, erect grower and hardy; fruit sweet, lucious, without a hard core; high flavor; jet black, small seeds; firm enough to ship and handle well. One of the largest sized berries.

Dewberries

Price of plants 10c each, 60c per dozen, $3.00 per hundred, $15.00 per thousand.

Austin's Improved—New from Texas; has been tested several years. Glossy shining black color; its very appearance has a tempting effect on those who see it. Its flavor is excellent. When fully ripe will melt in your mouth most pleasantly.

Lucretia — Perfectly hardy, remarkably productive; said to be the best of this class of fruit; ripens early, is often 1½ inches in length by 1 inch in diameter; sweet, lucious and melting; this variety is recommended most highly.

Mulberries

Price of Trees.

	Each	Per Doz.	Per 100
One year 6 to 8 ft.	$0.35	$3.00	$25.00
One year 5 to 6 ft.	.25	2.50	17.50
One year 4 to 5 ft.	.20	2.00	15.00

Black English (Morus Nigra)—Produces the largest and finest fruit; very productive; fruit black, very juicy, aromatic, with sub-acid flavor. Good for preserves. June to October.

Downings Everbearing—A beautiful tree for the lawn; bears an abundant supply of sweet, refreshing fruit for several weeks; berries are about one and one-half inches long; color blue-black.

Hick's Everbearing—Medium, very sweet and good; tree vigorous and profuse bearer. Season extends over three months.

Multicaulus or Silk Worm Mulberry—A strong growing small tree or giant shrub; fruit black and sweet.

Russian — A very hardy; rapid-growing timber tree of great value, especially in the West. Introduced by the Mennonites. Foliage abundant, and said to be very desirable in the culture of silk worms. Fruit of good size and produced in great abundance.

Stubbs—Large, two inches by three quarters, deep black, rich, sub-acid; extremely prolific. Valuable for the South. Georgia.

Pomegranates

Price of Trees.

	Each	Per Doz.	Per 100
One year 3 to 4 ft.	$0.35	$3.00	$25.00
One year 2 to 3 ft.	.20	2.00	15.00
One year 1½ to 2 ft.	.15	1.50	12.00

Papershell—Fruit very large. as large as the largest apple; eye very small; skin thin, pale yellow with crimson cheek; juice cells surrounding the seeds (the edible portion of the fruit) of the most magnificent crimson color, highly armoatic and very sweet. The Papershell is a fine grower, good bearer and ships well. October.

Purple Seeded.—Fruit as large as the largest apple; skin yellow with crimson blush pulp, deep rich crimson; very sweet and aromatic. Good bearer and shipper.

Sweet—Fruit large, with sweet, juicy pulp. Ripens in September.

16

Raspberries

Prices of plants except where noted, 10c each, 60c per dozen, $3.00 per hundred, $15.00 per thousand.

Cumberland (Black)—In hardiness and productiveness it is unexcelled by any other variety; berries are large and fine; quality very similar and fully equal to Gregg; fruit firm and will stand long shipments. Ripens midseason.

Cuthbert—Medium to large, conical, deep rich crimson; good quality; very firm, very hardy; season medium to late, unequestionably one of the best varieties for the market.

Gregg—Of good size, fine quality, very productive and hardy. Takes the same position among the black caps as Cuthbert among the red sorts. No one can afford to be without it.

King—Large, crimson; firm; flavor very good; hardy; a new variety; an abundant and early bearer.

Munger (Black)—Excels all others in size and productiveness five to eight days later than Gregg.

Miller (Red)—Dark red variety; makes many plants and requires thinning. Does well in many parts of the country.

Red Cardinal—A surprise in fullness of its merits—its growth, extreme hardiness and the exceeding productiveness of its choice, rich, pure flavored berries. Thrives where others fail; it will pay; it is not a novelty, but a variety of great merit.

Each, 15c; dozen, 75c; per hundred, $4.00.

St. Regis Everbearing—Variety said to produce fruit for four months. Brilliant crimson; good quality.

Each, 15c; dozen, $1.00; per hundred, $5.00.

Miller Raspberry.

Strawberries

Prices of Plants.

	Per 10	Per 50	Per 100	Per 1000	Per 10000
Aroma	$0.25	$0.60	$0.75	$3.50	$30.00
Improved Lady Thompson	.25	.50	.50	3.00	25.00
Klondyke	.25	.50	.60	3.00	25.00

Aroma—Standard variety, continues to be a favorite with many growers. Fruit large, bright red in color to the center. Delicious flavor, very productive and of firm texture; a good shipper and has a long fruiting season. Plant robust, foliage green.

Improved Lady Thompson—Well known Southern variety, where it is largely planted. Good plant maker and fairly productive of medium sized light colored fruit. It is early in ripening and lasts a long season. Seems to thrive and do best during a dry fruiting season, apparently the dryer the season the better it seems to do.

Klondyke—Fruit is of good size, though not extra large, but holds up well in size and lasts long season. Regular in shape, dark red in color and firm. In fact it is reported to carry extra well as a shipper. Probably no berry came so quickly to the front among Southern growers than this variety.

Miscellaneous Fruits

Paw-Paw—Grows best in thickets along river banks, attaining a height of 12 to 15 feet. Flowers of dark violet color. Fruit is cylindrical with obtuse ends three to five inches long, one to two inches thick, brown when fully ripe; flesh deep creamy yellow, soft and sweet. 50c each.

Black Haw (Viburnum prunifolium)—Small oval foliage, white flowers and black fruit. 25c each.

Red Haw—Deep green, glossy foliage, flowers large and white, fruit size of cherry. 25c each.

Parceley Haw—25c each.

Ground Huckleberry—A low ground bushy shrub, producing sweet blush berries. Fruit is solid in large quantities. 10c each, $1.00 per dozen, $5.00 per hundred.

Juneberry (Dwarf)—Grows four to six feet high; bunches out from the ground like currants; resembles the common Servis or Juneberry in leaf and fruit, but the fruit is larger, and in color almost black; commences to bear the second year after transplanting, and bears profusely. 25c each, $2.50 per dozen.

Wild Cherry (Prunus Virginiana)—Tree thirty feet tall, fruit size of peas, red or amber colored; puckery, stone smooth; when cultivated fruit is larger and fit for eating. Sometimes planted for ornaments. Generally hardy everywhere. 25c each, $2.50 per dozen.

17

Nut Bearing Trees

Pecans (Budded and Grafted)

Prices of Tree.

	Each	Per Doz.	Per 100
5 to 7 feet, extra	$2.00		
4 to 5 feet, strong	1.50	$12.00	$100.00
3 to 4 feet, strong	1.25	10.00	90.00
2 to 3 feet, strong	1.00	8.00	70.00
1½ to 2 feet, strong	.50	5.00	40.00

All our Pecan trees are grown from grafting and budding from bearing groves and are extra heavy rooted and dug carefully and packed so as to not injure in transit.

Alley—Medium size, shell thin, kernel is damp; flavor good; medium to heavy bearer, somewhat subject to scab under certain conditions.

Frotscher's Egg Shell—Large, very thin shell, kernel oily, plump, often dark colored, quality fair, popular in Georgia and Louisiana.

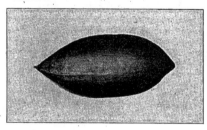

Mobile—Medium to large size; shell moderately thin; kernel usually plump; quality fair; flavor fair, very productive. Georgia.

Nelson—Size very large; shell thick, kernel generally plump, though often defective. Flavor good; very productive.

Pabst—Large; shell thick; kernel plump and sweet; productive but not very early.

Schley—From Jackson County, Miss. One of the best known and most widely disseminated varieties; medium to large, shell very thin; kernel plump; quality very rich; flavor fine.

Stuart—Large, roundish; thin shell; considerable corky growth in partitions; kernel plump; good quality. Mississippi.

Teche—Medium to small size. Shell medium to poor in flavor. Very productive and generally hardy over the entire south.

Van Deman—Large, oblong, thin shell; kernel not so plump as Stuart; flavor excellent. Mississippi.

Chestnuts

Sober Paragon Chestnut—Undoubtedly the best chestnut grown, but scarce. Large plantations of it are being established as a source of profit. It bears perfect nuts when but three years old, and nuts are as large as a silver half dollar. It is also hardy and vigorous and fruit is sweet and of the best quality.

5 to 6 ft. (Grafted),	$1.50
4 to 5 ft. (Grafted),	1.25
3 to 4 ft. (Grafted),	1.00

American Sweet Chestnut—The American Sweet Chesnut is much superior to both the European and Japanese kinds, although it does not, as yet, approach the size of either of them. Chesnuts are much easier to propagate than any other nut trees, and come into bearing earlier. It does not do well in limestone, or in wet boggy land. Nut is sweet and well flavored. Valuable shade tree for street or lawn.

6 to 8 feet extra heavy, $1.00 each.
4 to 6 feet extra heavy, .75 each.

Filberts

European Filberts—Succeeds well in all soils where the common hazel grows; fine for planting along timber belts, ravines and can also be used in shrubbery groups in parks and large grounds.

4 to 6 feet, $1.00 each.
3 to 4 feet, .40 each.

Walnuts

Black Walnuts (Juglans Nigra)—Common and stately forest tree in the Middle and Western states; grows from 40 to 60 feet high; has an open, spreading head and is rapid in growth; produces large crops of nuts with rough hard shell, containing rich oily kernels of fine flavor.

6 to 7 feet, $1.50 each.
4 to 6 feet, 1.00 each.
3 to 4 feet, .40 each.
2 to 3 feet, .25 each.

English Walnut (Madeira Nut—A fine and lofty growing tree with a handsome spreading head. Where hardy it produces immense crops of its thin-shelled delicious nuts which are always in demand at good prices. Not hardy enough for general culture in the North.

4 to 5 feet $0.75 each.
3 to 4 feet .50 each.
2 to 3 feet .30 each.
1½ to 2 feet .20 each.

Japanese Walnuts—Introduced from Japan, and are sure to prove of great importance in nut growing districts. Easily transplanted, hardy, abundant and early bearers. Comparatively little tap-root but plenty of laterals.

Cordiformis—This, as the name indicates, is heart shaped. Differs from the Sieboldi in form of the nuts, which are broad, pointed, flattened, somewhat resembling the shelbark hickory; meat large, of best quality, and easily removed as shell is thin and parts easily at the sutures, enabling one to get the kernel out whole. Flavor somewhat between that of the English walnut and Beech nut.

3 to 4 feet $0.50 each.
2 to 3 feet .40 each.

Sieboldi—If it produced no nuts, would be well worth cultivation for an ornamental tree. Nuts are borne in clusters of 12 or 15 at tips of previous season's branches. Have a smooth shell; thicker than the English, but not so thick as the Black Walnuts much resembling pecans. Meat is sweet, of good quality, flavor like a butternut, but less oily, commences bearing young, trees 3 to 4 years from nut in nursery rows frequently producing nuts.

1½ to 2 feet 25c each.

Ornamental Department

A great many people are beginning to realize that by expending a little time and study they can have well-kept and attractive grounds, adding to the beauty and comfort of the home and increasing the value of the property. If the grounds surrounding the house are extensive, beautiful effects can be produced by planting shade trees, shrubs, vines and flowers according to some pre-arranged plan. If the grounds are small, a few shrubs, such as the Altheas, Hydrangeas, Spireas and other sorts can be used to good advantage. Vines trained over porches, trellises, fences, etc., can be made very effective at a small cost and give great comfort and satisfaction not only to yourself, but your neighbors. Real estate owners who have vacant property to sell are beginning to plant fine trees and shrubs, knowing that they can secure a larger percentage on their investment when the ground is sold, as purchasers will pay more for a fine looking lot than one given over to unsightly surroundings. We would also emphasize the fact that you should **buy none but the best.** Few people realize the importance of getting started right. A little thought will convince you that it is not the quantity, but the quality that counts. Buy none but the best stock, properly grown by reliable nurserymen, who have given their best thought to the careful propagation and best varieties. We have a large stock of all kinds of shade trees, ornamental shrubs, etc., that has been selected with the greatest care and attention, both as to variety and quality.

Deciduous Trees

Maple, Silver Leaved or Soft (A. Dasy-Carpum)—A rapid growing tree of large size, irregular rounded form; foliage bright green above and silver beneath; attains about the same height or taller than the Norway. 10 to 12 ft., $1.00 each, $8.00 per dozen.

Maple, Ash-Leaved (Negunda fraxinifolium) (Box Elder) — Manitoba Maple. A native tree, maple-like in its seeds, and ash-like in foliage; of irregular spreading habit, and rapid growth. 8 to 10 ft., 75c each, $6.00 per dozen.

Maple, Norway (A. Platanoides)—A large, handsome tree with broad deep green foliage; has a very compact growth; attains a height of 100 feet; a valuable tree for parks, lawns or streets. 8 to 10 feet, $1.00 each, $10.00 per dozen.

Maple, Sugar or Hard (A. Saccharum)—A well known native tree, valuable both for the production of sugar and wood; very desirable as an ornamental shade tree. 8 to 10 feet, $1.00 each, $10.00 per dozen.

Red or Slippery Elm (Ulmus Fulva)—Not so large as the American, foliage larger and

19

Catalpa Bungei.

head more open; inner surface of bark used extensively for medicine. 10 to 12 feet, $1.00 each; 8 to 10 feet 75c each; 6 to 8 feet, 50c each.

Ash, American White (Fraxinus American)—A well known native tree; tall, very straight, with broad, round head and dense foliage. 10 to 12 feet, $1.00; 8. to 10 feet, 75c each.

American Sweet Gum or **Bilsted** (Liquidambar)—One of the finest American trees. Of medium size and moderate growth. Beautiful in all stages of growth, it is particularly handsome and striking in autumn, when the foliage turns to deep purplish crimson. 10 to 12 feet, $1.00 each; 8 to 10 feet, 75c each.

Tulip Tree or Whitewood (Liriodendron tulipifera)—A magnificent native tree, of tall, pyrimidal habit, with broad, glossy, fiddle-shaped leaves of a light green color, and beautiful tulip-like flowers. 10 to 12 feet, $1.00 each; 8 to 10 feet, 75c each.

Magnolia, Cucumber (M. acominata)—A beautiful native pyrimidal growing tree, attaining from 60 to 90 feet in height. Leaves 6 to 9 inches long, and bluish-green; flowers yellow, tinted with bluish-purple; fruit when green resembles a cucumber, hence the name. 4 to 6 feet, 50c each.

Texas Umbrella (Melia azedarach umraculiformis)—The first tree that came to notice was found near San Jacinto, Texas. Branches erect, and in a manner radiating from the trunk, the drooping foliage giving the tree appearance of an umbrella. Shade very dense; foliage bright dark green, produces lilac colored flowers, suceeded by a fruit with external pulp and hard nut

within. 5 to 6 feet, 75c each; 4 to 5 feet, 50c each; 3 to 4 feet, 25c each.

Catalpa, Chinese Bungi—A remarkable species forming a dense, round umbrella-like head; makes a beautiful lawn tree when grafted or budded on a high stem. Extra fine, $2.00 each, $22.00 per dozen.

Catalpa Speciosa—A variety which is said to have originated in the West; it is very hardy and a rapid grower and is being extensively planted for commercial purposes: has broad deep green leaves and beautiful large blossoms, making it a highly ornamental tree for lawn or street. Valuable for planting in groves for growing poles, posts and railroad ties. 6 to 8 feet, 60c each; 8 to 10 feet, 75c each.

Hackberry or Nettle Tree (Celtis Occidentalis)—A native tree that deserves more general planting. Leaves are light green, glossy, pointed. Not subject to insect pests. Branches are slender and grow horizontally, forming a wide shaped head. Thrives in all soils. 8 to 10 feet, 75c each.

Red Bud Cerisis Canadensis (American Judas)—A small tree of irregular rounded form, with pretty foliage and very showy when in bloom. Branches and twigs are covered with dense masses of small pink flowers in the fifth month before the leaves expand. Extra heavy, 10 to 12 feet, $1.50 each; 8 to 10 feet, $1.00 each; 6 to 8 feet, 50c each.

Weeping Mulberry.

Mulberry, Tea's Weeping (Morus)—The most graceful and hardy weeping tree in existence. Form a perfect shaped head, with long, slender, willowy branches, drooping to the ground. In light, airy gracefulness, delicacy of form and motion, it is without a rival. It has beautiful foliage, is hardy, safe and easy to transplant.. Admirably adapted for small or large grounds, or for cemetery planting. Strong trees budded on 6 to 7 feet heads, $2.00 each.

Black Gum (Nyssa sylvatica)—Leaves oval, 2 to 4 inches long; fruit nearly black, acid with ovoid stone, little flattened. Flowers in groups of two to fourteen. Native. 6 to 8 feet, 50c each; 4 to 6 feet, 25c each.

Sourwood (Oxydendrum arboreum)—Smooth barked tree, attaining a height of 60 feet; leaves oblong, 3 to 6 inches long, veiny, slender-stalked flowers on panicles of six or more racimes, bearing as many as two dozen small white tubular flowers. Valued for its highly colored autumn foliage. 6 to 8 feet, 50c each; 4 to 6 feet, 25c each.

Plane, Oriental (Platanus Orientalis)—A well-known tree, extensively used for street and park planting, especially in cities where there is much smoke. Nice trees, 50c each; $4.00 per dozen.

Poplar, Carolina (P. Monolifera)—Pyrimidal in form and vigorous in growth; leaves large, glossy, pale to deep green; valuable for street planting on account of its

Norway Maple.

Carolina Poplar.

rapid growth. 10 to 12 feet, 50c each; 8 to 10 feet, 35c each.

Poplar, Lombardy (Populus)—A native of Europe. Remarkable for its erect growth and tall spire-like form. 10 to 12 feet, 50c each; 8 to 10 feet, 35c each.

Prunus (Purple-Leaved Plum Pissardi)—A distinct and handsome little tree, covered with a mass of small, white, single flowers in spring; later with showy pinkish purple leaves that deepen in color to the end of the season. An unique lawn ornament at all times of the year. 4 to 5 feet, 50c each, 3 to 4 feet, 25c each.

Willow - Leaved Water Oak (Quercus Phellos)—Tree grows to a height of 60 feet with slender branches forming a conical head; leaves bright green and glossy. Acorn small and in a very shallow cup. A most beautiful tree for shade and ornament. 15 to 18 feet, $2.50 each; 10 to 12 feet, $2.00 each, 8 to 10 feet, $1.00 each.

Maiden Hair Tree or Salisburia (Ginko boloba)—About as handsome a small tree as can be cultivated. From Japan and grows into column about 40 feet high. Foliage is formed like the Adiantum fern, thick and glossy. It is largely used abroad for street planting and as an individual specimen is always handsome. Very desirable on small grounds. 6 to 8 feet 75c each; $7.00 per dozen.

Linden, American (Tilia Americana)—Grows about 60 feet high, rapid growing, large size, forming a broad round-topped head; leaves broadly oval, dark green above, light green underneath; flowers are creamy white, fragrant; a splendid street or lawn tree. 10 to 12 feet $1.50 each; 8 to 10 feet, $1.00 each.

Evergreens.

Evergreens

These take a prominent place in ornamental planting, giving a cheerful winter effect when deciduous trees are bare. They are especially useful as windbreaks, and for bleak and exposed situations, there being a wide range of choice among very hardy subjects. There are many rare and elegant conifers, whose first cost, however, is amply repaid by the pleasure of possessing a choice permanent specimen, but there is a long list of inexpensive varieties which will give the greatest satisfaction.

Coniferous Evergreens

(Cone Bearing Evergreens)

Abies Concolor (Colorado Silver Fir)—Regarded as the finest Rocky Mountain evergreen; foliage bluish above, silver beneath; habit of tree stately and distant; 'a e. 1 to 1½ feet, 50c each; 1½ to 2 feet, 75c each; 2 to 3 feet, $1.00 each.

Abies Douglasi (Douglas Spruce)—Horizontally spreading branches, conical form, light green leaves, glaucious beneath. 1½ to 2 feet, 75c each; 2 to 3 feet, $1.00 each; 3 to 4 feet, $1.50 each.

Larch, European (Larix Europea)—A native of the Alps of the South of Europe; an elegant growing, pyramidal tree; valuable for timber. 1½ to 2 feet, 50c each; 2 to 3 feet, 75c each; 3 to 4 feet, $1.50 each.

Picea alba (White Spruce)—70 feet. Native tree of the great northwest; foliage silvery gray exhaling a strong aromatic odor when bruised. Cones 1 to 2 inches long, glossy brown. 2 to 3 feet, 75c each; 3 to 4 feet, $1.00 each; 4 to 5 feet, $2.00 each.

Picea Engelmanni (Engleman's Spruce)—Another Colorado variety, resembling pungens with bluish green foliage. Makes fine specimen. 2 to 3 feet, 75c each; 3 to 4 feet, $1.25 each.

Spruce, Norway (Picea Excelsa)—A lofty, noble tree of perfect pyramidal habit, remarkably elegant and rich; as it gets age has fine, graceful, pendulous branches; it is exceedingly picturesque and beautiful. Very popular and deservedly so. One of the very best evergreens for hedges. 1½ to 2 feet, 50c each; 2 to 3 feet, 75c each; 3 to 4 feet, $1.00 each.

Norway Spruce.

22

Irish Juniper.

Spruce, Colorado Blue (Picea pungens glauca)—One of the hardiest and most beautiful of all the Spruces: in form and habit similar to the White Spruce; foliage of a rich blue or sage color. 1½ to 2 feet, 75c each; 2 to 3 feet, $1.00 each; 3 to 4 feet, $1.50 each.

Common Hemlock or Spruce (Tsuga Candensis)—Rapid growing and hardy tree which can be sheared into a bushy form making a fine hedge. Excellent for windbreaks or exposed situations. 1½ to 2 feet, 50c each, 2 to 3 feet, 75c each; 3 to 4 feet, $1.00 each.

American Arborvitae (Thuya occidentalis) —60 feet. Beautiful native species commonly known as the White Cedar; especially valuable for screens and hedges. Foliage bright green beneath, in winter assuming tones of brown or bronze. 5 to 6 feet, $1.00 each; 4 to 5 feet, 75c each; 3 to 4 feet, 50c each.

Chinese Arborvitae, Pyramidal (Thuya) —A densely branched variety forming a perfect column; holds its shape without trimming or pruning; hardy and will succeed anywhere the American Vitae does; a very ornamental type for many kinds of planting. 7 to 9 feet, $2.00 each; 5 to 7 feet, $1.50 each; 4 to 5 feet, $1.00 each; 3 to 4 feet, 75c each; 2 to 3 feet, 50c each.

Chinese Compacta Arborvitae (Thuya)— A dwarf, compact variety, with a conical head; bright green color; perfectly hardy, native of Japan. 1 to 1½ feet, 50c each; 2 to 2½ feet, 75c each: 2½ to 3 feet, $1.00 each.

Rosedale Arborvitae—1 to 1½ feet, 50c each; 1½ to 2 feet, 75c each; 2 to 3 feet, $1.00 each.

Pinus palustris (Southern Lumber Pine) —Tree about 100 feet with ascending branches forming an open head; winter buds, whitish, long; dark green leaves; cones dull brown, cylindric, 6 to 10 inches long; very important timber tree, hardy only in South. Rarely planted for ornaments. 1½ to 2 feet, 25c each; 2 to 3 feet, 50c each; 3 to 4 feet, $1.00 each.

Cedrus Atlantica (Mt. Atlas Cedar)—120 feet. Very handsome pyramidical tree with silvery green foliage, branches have an upright growing tendency and are very dense. Fine tree for the lawn. 1 to 1½ feet; 40c each; 1 to 2 feett, 60c each; 2 to 3 feet, $1.00 each.

Cedrus Leodara (Deodar)—Tall pyramidal tree, thick rigid bluish green foliage. One of the famous trees of the Himalayas. 1 to 1½ feet, 40c each; 1½ to 2 feet, 60c each; 2 to 3 feet, $1.00 each.

Taxus baccata (English Yew)—40 feet. A densely-branched, spreading bush of a dark, somber hue; one of the best evergreens for clipping into artificial forms. 3 to 4 feet, $1.50 each; 2 to 3 feet, $1.00 each.

Cypress Tree (Cupressus)—This number of our family of trees with aromatic foliage seem to adapt themselves to California conditions very well. Grow very well in the interior valleys; native habitation seems to be confined to California and the Gulf States. They are not particular in regard to soil and situation, but prefer deep sandy loams. 2 to 3 feet, $1.00 each; 1½ to 2 feet, 75c each.

Juniper, Irish (Juniperus Hibernica)—A distinct and beautiful variety, of erect, dense, conical outline, resembling a pillar of green; very desirable. 3 to 4 feet, $1.00 each; 2 to 3 feet, 75c each; 1½ to 2 feet, 50c each.

23

Miscellaneous Evergreens

Boxwood (Buxus)—These very ornamental shrubs of dense but ornamental growth, with shining foliage, are invaluable for grouping, lawn decoration and hedge purposes. For tub culture and for formal decorative work they are more extensively grown than any other plants. They thrive in a warm, dry climate fully as well on the coast. 6 to 12 inches, 10c each; $1.00 per dozen, $7.50 per hundred.

English Laurel (Laurus cerasus)—Southern Europe to Northern Persia. 10 to 15 feet high. Fine large evergreen with broad shining leaves; produces large panicles of creamy white flowers followed by purple berries. 2 to 3 feet, $1.00 each; 18 to 24 inches, 75c each.

Privet, Amoor River (Ligustrum Amurense)—A valuable ornamental shrub for hedges and borders; very hardy; foliage glossy green and holds its color almost the entire year; will stand shearing to any extent. 10c each, $1.00 per dozen, $3.50 per fifty, $6.00 per hundred, $50.00 per thousand.

Camelia Japonica—Very beautiful flowering evergreens; their handsome dark green foliage and magnificent wax-like flowers which appear in great profusion all winter render them indispensible for the conservatory and well adapted for parlor and window culture; perfectly hardy in this climate. All colors, 1½ to 2 feet, $1.25 each; 1 to 1½ feet, $1.00 each.

Magnolia Grandiflora (Bull Bay)—80 feet. Most noble of American evergreens; foliage is thick; brilliant green on the upper surface and rusty underneath; flowers are pure waxy white and of immense size and very fragrant. Nicely headed trees, 5 to 6 feet, $1.00 each; 3 to 4 feet, 75c each; 2 to 3 feet 50c each.

Ligustrum (California Privet)—Has broad oval shaped leaves which remain on well into the winter. One of the most universal of hedge plants and one of the best, growing especially well at the seashore. 10c each, $1.00 per dozen, $2.50 per fifty, $4.00 per hundred, $30.00 per thousand.

Hardy Perennial Plants

Day Lily (Funkia)—A superb autumn flower, having broad, light green leaves, prettily veined, and long, trumpet-shaped pure white flowers, that possess a delightful, though delicate fragrance. 15c each, $1.50 per dozen.

Iris, German (Germanica) — This group blooms in May with wonderful combinations of coloring; leaves broad sword-like. We have an assortment of the best sorts. 15c each, $1.50 per dozen, $10.00 per hundred.

Iris, Japan (Kaempferi)—The Japanese Iris should be planted in a somewhat cool, moist situation, and in rich soil. Its flowers, in late June and July, are quite distinct from those of all the varieties and will compare favorably with some of the exotic orchids. We have a good assortment of the best varieties. 15c each, $1.50 per dozen, $10.00 per hundred.

Paeonies, Herbaceous—Are among the most showy and useful of hardy plants. They are all hardy and admirably adapted to the climate of most of our states, growing well in almost any situation of soil. We offer a splendid assortment. White, pink and red, 25c each, $2.50 per dozen.

Rhodendron Catawbiense—Shrub. 6 to 10 feet high, leaves round at base, oval to oblong; flowers lilac purple, about 1½ inches across. One of the most beautiful native shrubs. Hardy as far north as New England. June. 12 to 18 inches, $1.00 each; $10.00 per dozen.

Yucca, Filamentosa (Adam's Needle)—Among hardy ornamental foliage and flowering plants this can be classed at the head of the list. Its broad, sword-like foliage and tall branched spikes of large, fragrant, drooping, creamy white flowers make it an effective plant for all positions; 5 to 6 feet high. 25c each, $2.50 per dozen.

Yucca.

Deciduous Shrubs

Althea (Hibiscus Syriacus) — Rose of Sharon. One of the most showy and beautiful shrubs. Flowers large, double, of many brilliant colors. Blooms freely in August and September when few other trees or shrubs are in blossom. Four colors, 3 to 4 feet, 35c each; $3.50 per dozen.

Almond, Double Rose-flowering (Prunus Japonica rubra fl. pl)—A beautiful small shrub, bearing in May before the leaves appear, small, double rose-like flowers, closely set upon the twigs. 25c each.

Almond, Double White-flowering (Prunus Japonica rubra fl. pl.)—Produces beautiful white flowers in May. 25c each.

Azalea (Ghent, Pontica)—A splendid assortment of hybrids averaging a little larger in size and showing greater diversity of color-shades than other Azaleas. Delightfully fragrant. Choice named varieties, well set with flower buds. Mixed colors, 2 to 3 feet clumps, $1.50 each.

Barberry, Purple-leaved (Berberis purpurea)—Foliage and fruit of a violet-purple color, very striking; fine for single specimens; also a desirable ornamental hedge plant, planted by itself or intermingled with the common. 35c each, $2.50 per dozen, $20.00 per 100.

Calycanthus. Sweet-Scented Shrub (Floridus)—A native species with double purple flowers, very fragrant and the wood is also fragrant; foliage rich dark green; blooms in June and at intervals afterward. 25c each. n

Citrus, Trifoliata (Trifoliate Orange)—A small tree, with strong, stiff thorns; fruit golden-yellow, about size of a walnut, cov-

Althea.

ered with short hairs, pulp rather dry, sour and bitter, sometimes used for preserves. Largely used for hedges. Strong plants, 25c each; $2.00 per dozen; $12.50 per 100.

Cornus, Florida (White-Flowering Dogwood)—An American species, of spreading irregular form, growing from 16 to 20 feet high. Flowers are produced in spring before the leaves appear. They are white and very showy. Popular. 4 to 6 feet, 25c each.

Crape Myrtle (Lagerstroemia)—A very strong growing shrub; adapting itself to almost any soil condition, should have a place in every garden. Leaves are bright green, retaining their fresh color all summer; flowers are produced in large panicles at the ends of the branches during the entire summer. They are very petty, having curiously crimpd petals. Should be winter-pruned to retain compactness of form. White, crimson and pink, 2 to 3 feet, 50c each; 1½ to 2 feet, 35c each.

Deutzia—Double-flowered, a hardy shrub with luxuriant foliage and beautiful flowers; produced late in June on long racemes; white tinged with pink and very double. White and pink, 35c each.

Euonymus, Burning Bush (Atropurpureus)—An ornamental evergreen shrub or small tree. Leaves are long and narrow, of a purplish color. Flowers are purple and borne in clusters; blooms in June, followed by small scarlet berries. 25c each, $2.50 per dozen.

Forsythia, Fortune's Fortunelii (Golden Bell)—Growth upright, foliage deep green, flowers bright yellow. 25c each.

Deutzia.

Hydrangea.

Lilac, Purple (S. Vulgaris)—The well-known purple variety; always a standard sort. 3 to 4 feet, 40c each; 2 to 3 feet, 35c each; 1½ to 2 feet, 25c each.

Lilac, White (S. Vulgaris alba)—Flowers white and fragrant. 3 to 4 feet 40c each; 2 to 3 feet, 35c each; 1½ to 2 feet, 25c each.

Silver Bell or Snowdrop (Halesia)—Brown light green foliage, dense growing trees of small size and well adapted for lawn culture. Chaste pure white flowers are produced in abundance along the entire length of the branches as the leaves appear in spring, and give a very charming picture. Best grown in well drained soil in somew a sheltered position. 25c each, $2.50 per dozen.

Hardy Hydrangea (H. Paniculata grandiflora)—A beautiful tall shrub with leaves of bright shiny green; flowers borne in panicles from 8 to 12 inches long. thick pink, changing to brown later in the fall. Blooms in August and September; can be

grown in tree forms successfully and makes a very desirable lawn ornament. Strong plants, 40c each, $3.50 per dozen.

Cape Jasmine (Gardenia jasminoides)—A very pretty shrub with thick evergreen foliage and large double waxy camellia-like fragrant flowers blooming from May to September. 35c each; $3.50 per dozen.

Spiraea Thunbergii (Thunberg's Spiraea) —Of dwarf habit, rounded, graceful form; branches slender and somewhat drooping; foliage narrow and yellowish green; flowers small, white, appearing early in spring, being one of the best Spiraeas to flower. Esteemed on account of its neat, graceful habit. Extra heavy plants, 50c each, $4.00 per dozen.

Spiraea Van Houtte—The grandest of the Spiraeas. It is a beautiful ornament for the lawn at any season, but when in flower it is a complete fountain of white bloom, the foliage hardly showing. Clusters of twenty to thirty flat, white florets make up the racemes. Perfectly hardy and an early bloomer. Extra heavy plants, 50c each; $4.00 per dozen.

Snow Ball, Common (Viburnum Opulus Sterilis)—An old and well-known shrub, bearing large balls of pure white flowers. 3 to 4 feet, 50c each; 2 to 3 feet, 35c each; 1½ to 2 feet, 25c each.

Weigelia (Diervilla)—Beautiful shrubs that bloom in June and July. Flowers are produced in so great a profusion as to almost hide the foliage. They are very desirable for the border or for grouping and also for specimen plants for the lawn. White, carmine-red and crimson, strong plants, 40c each.

Snowball.

Climbers and Trailers

Clematis.

Ampelopsis (American Ivy or Virginia Creeper) (A. quinquefolia)—One of the finest vines for covering walls, verandas or trunks of trees; foliage green, turning to a rich crimson in autumn; a rapid grower and quickly fastens to anything it touches. 25c each, $2.50 per dozen.

Ampelopsis Veitchii (Japan Ivy)—Leaves smaller than the American; forms a dense sheet of green as the leaves overlap each other; is a little difficult to start, but when once established, requires no further care; foliage changes to crimson scarlet in the fall, very valuable for covering brick or stone structures, rockeries or walls, etc. 15c each, $1.50 per dozen.

Trumpet Vine (Jasminum)—Beautiful and very showy evergreen climbers and with a little care and an occasional application of manure, will more than repay in their appearance the care bestowed on them. 25c each, $2.50 per dozen.

Clematis paniculata (Japanese Clematis)—A very hardy climber, introduced from Japan, with fragrant, small white flowers, in clusters; completely covering the upper portion of the vine in late summer and early autumn. Does well in a sunny situation. Will stand severe pruning during the winter. Extra strong plants, 50c each; strong plants, 25c each.

Yellow Jasmine (Jasminum)—These are very interesting plants, some of them growing in the form of shrubs while others are either climbers or trailing plants. Very graceful and their mass of showy flowers which in some varieties push out the full length of the stems, makes them attractive. Strong plants, 15c each, $1.50 per dozen, $10.00 per hundred.

Wistaria, Chinese Purple (W. Sinensis)—One of the best of the Wistarias, rapid growing and elegant, attaining 15 to 20 feet in a season; flowers a pale-blue, borne in long pendulous clusters in May and June. Extra heavy plants, 35c each, $4.00 per dozen, medium size plants, 25c each, $2.50 per dozen.

Climbing Roses

Prices of Climbing Roses: 35c each, $4.00 per dozen, 2 dozen for $7.00, our selection.

Wm. Allen Richardson—Large, full flowers of coppery yellow, tinged with carmine; has a delicious fragrance. Produces flowers very freely and on account of its unique color, is greatly admired.

Gainsborough—Rosy flesh color, tinged with salmon.

Climbing Wooton—Hybrid Tea. A sport from the famous rose Souvenir de Wooton, and identical with it, except that it is a strong rampant climber producing in wonderful profusion, superbly formed flowers with thick leathery petals. As a climbing rose, it will rank among the best,

Climbing Meteor—Hybrid Tea. Climbing Meteor is the acme of all red climbing roses. It is a free, persistent bloomer and will make a growth of from ten to fifteen feet a season. At the head of the list of all roses for summer blooming, loaded with deep rich flowers all the time.

Climbing Malmaison—Color rich creamy-flesh, shaded clear pearly rose.

Reine Marie Henriette—Very large, beautiful deep cherry-red flowers. Commonly called the Red Gloire de Dijon. Very beautiful and one of the grandest tender climbers. Hardy with slight protection.

Marchal Niel—This variety is well known and considered to be one of the most magnificent roses in existence. Flowers are pure, deep yellow, and its fragrance delicious. This is the most popular everblooming climbing rose in existence. It is not hardy in the North.

Mrs. Robert Peary—White Climbing Kaiserin Augusta Victoria. One of the very best of this class, strong vigorous grower. Flowers extra large and sweet; color rich creamy white, delicately tinted with lemon. Blooms constantly the whole season.

Elie Beauvillian—Lovely salmon color.

Roses

Prices, 25c each, $2.50 per dozen, 2 dozen for $4.50, our selection.

Clothilde Soupert—Medium size; very double and beautifully imbricated like an aster; produced in clusters; pearly white, with rosy lake centers, liable to vary, producing often red and white flowers on same plant.

Killarney Rose.

White Maman Cochet—A splendid rose; has all the good qualities of Maman Cochet. Like some other white roses, this variety, especially in the autumn, shows pink markings on the outside petals when the flower is in bud.

Bessie Brown—Bears large full flowers of extraordinary depth and fullness and is deliciously sweet; color pure white clouded and flushed with pure pink.

Etoile de Lyon—Color is pure bright yellow; makes beautiful buds and is very double and sweet.

Mrs. B. R. Cant—Clear bright rose-red, elegantly shaded.

Cherry Ripe—Light cherry crimson; full and globular. Very fragrant.

White Killarney—In form, size and freedom of bloom this rose is the same as the famous Killarney pink, of which it is a sport, but it is more double and the flowers are pure waxy white.

Paul Neyron—One of the most desirable garden roses known; also considered the largest; color a deep rose-pink; very fragrant; hardy and a strong grower.

Helen Gould—Color is rich, vinous crimson. Flowers are large, perfectly double, deliciously sweet.

Pink Maman Cochet—This is our favorite rose. It is one of the largest size, the flower is built up or rounded and very double; the color is a deep, rosy pink, the inner side of the petals being a silvery rose, shaded and touched with golden yellow.

Meteor—Rich, velvety crimson. Very vivid and striking. Remarkable for its vivid color.

Kaiserin Augusta Victoria—White, faintly blended with cream color, very large, full and double, almost perfect in form and continues beautiful even when fully expanded.

Killarney—One of the most beautiful roses grown, strong, vigorous, perfectly hardy and in every way a rose that should be more cultivated; flowers are very large, buds long and pointed. Color a brilliant shining pink; one of the best Tea varieties.

General MacArthur—Color bright glowing crimson-scarlet, vigorous grower, every shoot producing a flower, intense, brilliant color. Unexcelled as a splendid garden rose.

Catherine Mermet—Extra fine; light rose-color, a vigorous grower; large, double and very fragrant.

White La France—A seedling of La France, extra large, full, deep pearly white flowers, delicately shaded with soft rose; exquisitely beautiful and delightfully fragrant.

Etoile de France—Crimson. Makes beautiful large pointed buds, extra large, fully double flowers, 3½ to 4½ inches across. Color intense brilliant crimson, very fragrant.

Pink La France—This is probably the most popular rose in cultivation. Both buds and flowers are of lovely form and grand size, exceedingly sweet; color fine peach blossom, elegantly clouded with rosy flesh. Begins to bloom while very small and continues bearing until stopped by freezing weather.

Mme. Jules Grolez—China rose passing to clear rich satiny pink; fine.

Kaiserin Auguste Victoria.

ORDER SHEET

The CURETON NURSERIES, Austell, Ga.

AMOUNT ENCLOSED

....
(Very Plainly)

fice.. *P. O. Box* ....

.... *State*....................

.... *Forward by*....................

Office ....

Station ....

Company ....

d..

P. O. or Express Order, $..................

Draft ⸱   ⸱   ⸱ $..................

Cash ⸱   ⸱   ⸱ $..................

Postage Stamps ⸱ $..................

TOTAL, ⸱ $..................

Date ....191......

> **VERY IMPORTANT** — No difference how often you have written us, always give your full Address and write your Name, Post Office, County and State very plainly.

Do you wish us to substitute to the best of our judgment in case any varieties or sizes red should be exhausted? Write **Yes or No,**.........................
Please write in the quantity, full name of variety, size or age and price. Any necessary spondence should be written on a separate sheet.

Y	FULL NAME OF VARIETY	SIZE OR AGE	PRICE

QUANTITY	FULL NAME OF VARIETY	SIZE OR AGE	PRICE

TABLE OF CONTENTS